A to Z Devotions for Writers

By

Pamela D. Williams

A to Z Devotions for Writers

CrossLink Publishing
www.crosslinkpublishing.com

Copyright © 2013 Pamela D. Williams
All rights reserved. No part of this book may be reproduced in any form, except for brief quotations in reviews, without the written permission of the author.

Printed in the United States of America. All rights reserved under International Copyright Law.

ISBN 978-1-936746-52-1

Library of Congress Control Number: 2013937750

All scripture quotations in this publication are from the Good News Translation – Second Edition. Copyright © 1992 by American Bible Society. Used by permission.

Cover inkwell image by Lily Mackay.
(http://www.dancaster.com/lilymackay.htm) Used by permission.

Acknowledgments

"*I* thank my God for you every time I think of you. . . ."
—Philippians 1:3

Special thanks to my husband, Dick, who heads up my cheering section. He is a well-spring of encouragement to me in my writing endeavors and I am blessed beyond measure to be his wife.

Thank you to Arlee Bird for following God's nudge and setting forth the "Blogging from A to Z April Challenge".

My sincere appreciation goes to Dawn Hamsher, Cheryl Andreus, Brianna Renshaw, and Virginia Jelinek who tirelessly edited *A to Z Devotions for Writers*. I truly could not have done it without their sharp eyes and strong writing skills.

I am grateful to writer and artist, Lily Mackay, who allowed the graphic designers to feature her beautiful inkwell on the cover.

Thanks to Rick Bates who rendered the intimidating process of publishing into simple and painless steps I could handle.

And most importantly, I thank God for the incredible gift of allowing me to be, as Mother Teresa describes it, "a little pencil" in His hand.

"I planted the seed, Apollos watered the plant, but it was God who made the plant grow. The one who plants and the one who waters really do not matter. It is God who matters, because he makes the plant grow."
1 Corinthians 3:6-7

Pam Williams

TABLE OF CONTENTS

Acknowledgments iii
Foreword vii
Gleaning the most from *A to Z Devotions for Writers* ix
A is for Ages: Writing is for Everyone 1
B is for Bible: Writing from God's Word 5
C is for Call: Writing is a Call from God 9
D is for Diversity: Writing Notes or Writing Novels 11
E is for Editing: Writing Requires Our Best 15
F is for First: Writing within God's Priorities 19
G is for Gardening: Writing to Plant and Water 23
H is for Hook: Writing to Catch a Reader 27
I is for Inspiration: Writing Wellsprings 31
J is for Journals: Writing from Day to Day 35
K is for Kindred: Writing Buddies 37
L is for Light: Writing to Draw Others to Jesus 41
M is for Memoirs: Writing for the Next Generation 43
N is for No: Writing in the Face of Rejection 47
O is for Overcome: Writing, Over, Under, and Through 51
P is for Prayer: Writing in the Power of Prayer 53
Q is for Quiet: Writing in the Secret Place 57
R is for Reading: Writing Requires Reading 61

S is for Submissions: Writing for Publication 63
T is for Testimony: Writing to Witness 67
U is for Urgent: Writing is Crucial 71
V is for Voice: Writing from Within 73
W is for Words: Writing Wields Power... 75
X is for Explicable: Writing to be Understood 79
Y is for Yearn: Writing Goals 83
Z is for Zest: Writing with Pizazz 85
ABOUT THE AUTHOR 89

Foreword

The ugly twins of Fear and Self-Doubt raise their alarming heads and roar at every writer. Plagued by the menacing silence of Writers' Block and frenzied by the unstoppable scurrying of Time, how do Christian writers tame these snarling beasts?

Typically, believers turn to God's Word as both shield and sword against such foes. We discover direction through the Scriptures, draw peace from conversations with Jesus, and are encouraged by the words and experiences of others. Devotional books offer all of these elements, usually tailored to a specific reader—mothers, golfers, teens, cat lovers, couples, etc.

In 2010, using Marlene Bagnull's *Write His Answer: A Bible Study for Christian Writers*, I birthed and facilitated a writers' inspiration and critique group. I searched bookstores, workshops, and the Internet for devotionals for writers that I could use to open our meetings. The choices were few. Out of necessity, I began writing devotionals to open our writers' Bible study.

In April of 2011, I participated in Arlee Bird's (Lee Jackson) A to Z Blogging Challenge. God led me to write meditations for the challenge. I discovered many of them spoke to the hearts of writers. A year later, *A to Z Devotions for Writers* took shape.

A to Z Devotions for Writers is a resource that will meet the specific spiritual needs of those who want their writing to minister to others. Covering each letter of the alphabet, these devotionals offer pertinent scripture readings, a meditation focused on various aspects of the writing life, a short relevant prayer and "block" busting writing applications. Written to inspire, encourage, challenge, instruct, reassure, comfort and motivate writers, these devotionals will not only drive pen to paper but will illuminate how writers can apply God's truths to their writing.

Gleaning the most from *A to Z Devotions for Writers*

Do you ever find yourself simply going through the motions of "doing" devotions? At times I have read through an entire meditation and at the end, realized that I could not identify the author's main point because I wasn't really giving the devotional my full attention.

With just a few intentional steps you can glean a bit more from the devotionals included in *A to Z Devotions for Writers*:

- Pray before you start. Ask God to speak to you through His Word and through the devotional. Be open to the movement of His Holy Spirit during these moments with Him.

- Read the scripture aloud. What do you hear God saying through the chosen passage?

- After reading the meditation, write one sentence that sums up the main point of the lesson. How does it apply to you as a writer or to your current work in progress?

- Pray within the focus of the suggested prayer.

- Write from the prompt. This will get your creative juices flowing and may just lead to a story or an article that you could submit for publication. Write no less than 100 words for each prompt.

A is for Ages: Writing is for Everyone

> "I will pour out my Spirit on everyone. Your sons and daughters will proclaim my message; your young men will see visions, and your old men will have dreams."
>
> —Acts 2:17

Read: Psalm 148:7-13

Does age matter when it comes to writing? Can we be too old or too young to write? Some of us might think so.

Despite the desire, writers in their retirement years often suffer from the "terrible too-s"—it's *too* late in life to start writing; I'm *too* slow to learn the ins and outs of submitting; I'm *too* tired to tackle a full-length book project.

Yet, God recognizes there is wisdom that comes with age. (Job 12:12) Using life experiences as the basis for stories, seniors can leave a legacy of lessons learned at life's knee.

Many authors have proven we are never too old to write—Jan Karon published her first book at age 59; Laura Ingalls Wilder began the classic

Pamela D. Williams

Little House books at the age of 65; and Gilbert Morris has written over 200 books since he turned 57.

Doubts about writing abilities afflict more than just older adults. Young writers also battle the "terrible too-s"—I'm too inexperienced; there are too many writing rules to learn; I'm too busy juggling my education, job, and family life.

Ever the potter, God sees potential and pliability in young writers. Jesus said, "Father, Lord of heaven and earth! I thank you because you have shown to the unlearned what you have hidden from the wise and learned." (Matthew 11:25)

Consider Dallas Woodburn, who published her first book in the 5th grade and sold 900 copies just through friends and relatives! Tessa Emily Hall, author of *Purple Moon*, was offered a publishing contract at the age of 16. Alexa Schnee, 18, is the author of *Shakespeare's Lady*, and the youngest recipient ever of the Mount Hermon "Most Promising Writer" Award.

When we allow God to be our mentor, all stages of life can contain advantages for writing.

Prayer: Lord, make clear to me the benefits this juncture in time holds for my writing. Amen.

Writing Application: Contemplate a lesson you recently learned from someone close your current age. Write about where, when, what and how it impacted your life, as well as a character sketch of the person from whom you learned the lesson.

B is for Bible: Writing from God's Word

> "The word of God is alive and active, sharper than any double-edged sword. It cuts all the way through, to where soul and spirit meet, to where joints and marrow come together. It judges the desires and thoughts of the heart."
>
> —Hebrews 4:12

Read: Psalm 19:7-11

"The B-I-B-L-E—yes, that's the book for me. I stand alone on the Word of God, the B-I-B-L-E."

Do you remember this little ditty? I sang it nearly every Sunday as a child at St. Luke's Lutheran Church. I later taught it to my children and grandchildren, because, though simple, the words share important truths—truths writers can count on.

First, the Bible is the Word of God. In 2 Timothy 3:16-17 we learn that "All Scripture is inspired by God and is useful for teaching the truth, rebuking error, correcting faults, and giving instruction for right living, so that the person who serves God may be fully qualified and equipped to do every kind of good deed."

Allowing God's Word to permeate our own lives first is vital if we want to pen words that God can use to change others.

Second, we can stand on the Bible as the basic guidebook for our faith. When I listen with my full attention, Jesus uses my time in God's Word to instill new perspectives, to communicate greater understanding, and to provide motivation for me to take action. He then helps me to pass these insights on to my readers.

Third, the Bible is the book for me, for you, for all of us. Why did God give us the Bible? God had His Word written down so that we may believe that Jesus is the Messiah, the Son of God, and that through our faith in him we can have life. Writing is a tool we can use to share with others the Good News of salvation that we read in God's Word.

Joshua 1:8 challenges us to study the Bible day and night. What better book is there to prepare us for writing than the one that offers us life in all its fullness?

Prayer: Dear God, light my way through your Word and guide me to the verses that will direct my steps. Amen.

Writing Application: Choose one of the following Bible verses and write how you feel it applies to writing as a ministry: Psalm 102:18, Habakkuk 2:2, 1 Corinthians 11:12.

C is for Call: Writing is a Call from God

> "God has made us what we are, and in our union with Christ Jesus he has created us for a life of good deeds, which he has already prepared for us to do."
>
> —Ephesians 2:10

Read: Isaiah 44:21

Who prompted you to begin writing? For me, God used Gladys Taber's down-to-earth writing about her everyday life—her farm, garden, pets and cooking to nudge me to try writing about my cats. Later, God gently pushed me toward writing for Christian publications.

One of the most life-changing truths I learned about writing is that it can be a call to ministry. In reality, it is God who beckons us to write for Him. While others may influence us to write, Ephesians 2:10 tells us it is God who creates and calls us to write.

"God . . . calling me?" you ask.

Yes! In Matthew 28:19 God instructs all believers to share the "Good News". Though we may doubt ourselves, God has granted writers the ability to craft thoughts into words that will draw and nurture others in their relationship with God.

Since only a minority of the world's general population read strictly Christian books and articles, we are also called to minister to people through our secular writing. C. S. Lewis said, "What we want is not more little books about Christianity, but more little books by Christians on other subjects—with their Christianity 'latent'."

How are you answering the call? Have you heard God softly whispering, "Write for me"? If so, be assured; God will equip you for the task He has already prepared for you to do.

Prayer: Father, I thank you for calling me to minister through the gift of writing. I am your servant, Lord. Use me. Amen.

Writing Application: Make a list of areas in which you are knowledgeable or possess a keen interest—anything you have studied or experienced or are curious about. These will most likely be topics about which God will call you to write. File this list for future story and article ideas.

D is for Diversity: Writing Notes or Writing Novels

> "There are different abilities to perform service, but the same God gives ability to all for their particular service. The Spirit's presence is shown in some way in each person for the good of all."
>
> —1 Corinthians 12:6-7

Read: 1 Corinthians 12:12-27

What was that instrument the band director was holding up?

"Students, this is an E-flat alto clarinet," announced Mr. Spayd. "Fingered just like the B-flat soprano clarinet, it strengthens harmonic scoring. I would like to add a few altos to our woodwind section. Anybody interested? See me after class."

Since I sang alto in chorus, the alto clarinet appealed to me. Much to Mr. Spayd's delight, I fell in love with the instrument, practicing several hours every day.

"Alto" describes my personality. I like joining with, supporting, and contributing to the efforts of others—in life, in the church, and in writing.

Pamela D. Williams

Sometimes we feel that we are less talented or our work is less important than that of other writers. We think well-known authors, whose endeavors put them in the limelight, are more vital to the ministry of writing. However, like in a band, everyone's part counts.

Early Christians obviously wrestled with insecurities about their spiritual value. Both Romans 12 and 1 Corinthians 12 emphasize that God has purposefully gifted each of us, knowing a diversity of strengths, passions, and abilities will minister more effectively.

In the ministry of writing my role is often supportive—reporting on church events for the local newspaper, writing stories for Sunday school take-home papers, contributing to anthologies, and posting encouraging content on my blog. These writing opportunities are seldom "center stage", yet they undoubtedly serve God and His people.

Without writers for The Upper Room or Secret Place, millions of people would miss out on daily spiritual guidance; there would be no Chicken Soup for the Soul series without inspiring stories from contributors. Though God sometimes asks us to work in supportive, "behind-the-scenes" roles, it doesn't make our offerings less significant, just less visible.

Prayer: Lord, help me not to compare myself with others, but instead to realize the importance of the writing tasks you give me. Amen.

A to Z Devotions for Writers

Writing Application: Think about the different parts of the human body. As a writer, which do you identify with the most? Do you see yourself as a mouth or a heart? A kidney or an index finger? Explain why you identify with the part.

E is for Editing: Writing Requires Our Best

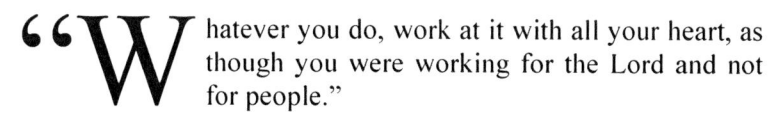

> "Whatever you do, work at it with all your heart, as though you were working for the Lord and not for people."
>
> —Colossians 3:23

Read: 2 Timothy 2:15

"Ugh! I'm in the editing and revision stage of my book and I keep procrastinating. It is just so overwhelming," my friend Dawn lamented.

I could commiserate with her. After editing my how-to book on creating meaningful worship for high school Baccalaureate services I didn't want to read the word "Baccalaureate" for a very long time.

So how do we motivate ourselves to tackle this unappealing but necessary task? Colossians 3:23 urges us to do our best, just like we would if we were editing a piece to present to God. As believers called by the Lord to write, we ARE writing for Him! The words that we write are at His bidding and for His purposes. Editing can only better what we have written for Him.

Pamela D. Williams

A good job of editing usually takes about as long as the initial creative writing process and requires considerably more patience. However, the writing quality, clarity, readability, organization and cohesiveness of our manuscript will be greatly improved—allowing us to offer God and our readers our very best.

Here are just a few guidelines to get us started on the editing process:

- Pray about this stage of writing.

- Let the manuscript rest for a while, but no more than a month.

- Read your work aloud.

- Listen to someone else read it aloud.

- Edit when you are refreshed. For most people this is in the morning.

- Ask a writer-friend to be your editing partner.

- "Edit ruthlessly," advises Malcolm Forbes. "Words are a lot like inflated money – the more of them that you use, the less each one of them is worth. Go through your entire [manuscript] just as many times as it takes. Search out and annihilate all unnecessary words, and sentences – even entire paragraphs."

Prayer: Father, you deserve my best. Please give me the steadfastness and motivation to thoroughly edit my work. Amen.

Writing Application: Choose one of your older, unpublished manuscripts. Edit it as Forbes recommends—ruthlessly.

F is for First: Writing within God's Priorities

> "Be concerned above everything else with the Kingdom of God and with what he requires of you, and he will provide you with all these other things."
>
> —Matthew 6:33

Read: Matthew 22:37-38

The money tempted me. As payment for my story, an anthology publisher offered me more than twice as much as I had received for my first stand-alone book! While I'll admit the story fit the theme of the anthology perfectly and would probably touch many hearts with its Christian message, I hesitated. The publisher frowned on changing the characters names and would not allow me to use a pseudonym. However, for me to take credit as the author and use the real names of the people in the story would create strife within the neighborhood where I grew up.

As Christians, our first priority is to live in a way that pleases God—and that includes our writing. But what guidelines can we follow, especially in cases like the one I shared, to keep God first in our writing? A litmus test of five Scriptures may help.

1. "Keep watch, and pray that you will not fall into temptation." (Mark 14:38)

   Has my writing project been covered in prayer? Have I sought the Lord's leading and input?

2. "Create in me a pure heart, O God, and renew a steadfast spirit within me." (Psalm 51:10)

   Are my motives for writing and/or publishing the story pure and honorable?

3. "Love one another warmly as Christians, and be eager to show respect for one another." (Romans 12:10)

   Does the article show respect? Will this story be hurtful to a person, a relationship, a ministry?

4. "Study God's Word day and night . . ." (Joshua 1:8)

   Does what I have written uphold scriptural principles?

5. "Fill your minds with those things that are good and that deserve praise: things that are true, noble, right, pure, lovely, and honorable." (Philippians 4:8)

   Is my article free of spite? Is it honorable? Does it stretch the truth?

If we measure our work against these standards, our writing will honor God and benefit others.

Prayer: Lord, help me to set aside my ambitions and honor your Word with mine. Amen.

Writing Application: Pick one of the listed Scriptures and write about how it applies to your current work in progress.

G is for Gardening: Writing to Plant and Water

"For we are partners working together for God, and you are God's field."

—1 Corinthians 3: 9

Read: 1 Corinthians 3:5-9

As writers we can spiritually plant and water for Jesus through our writing. Sometimes we are the ones with the little packet of faith seeds scattering a few here and a few there. Others times we are urged to carry watering cans of encouragement to sprinkle on thirsty sprouts of belief. Either task is a holy privilege.

Just a simple comment on a blog post or a story shared in a devotional booklet can plant a seed of faith in the life of one who does not fully understand God's plan of salvation or who is struggling to live the Christian life. Often as we garden for God in our writing we are unaware of how our words are impacting others. Occasionally, God grants us a glimpse of the fruit our "sowing" and "watering" has helped to produce.

Long ago I was a camp counselor for 4th to 6th grade girls. Counselors were responsible for bedtime devotions and I liked to write my own meditations from passages God had used to speak to me. The girls seemed to enjoy them and discussion always followed.

Years later I opened the mail and found a bulletin from a United Methodist church in our Susquehanna Conference. Turning to the back, I read the name of the minister, Pastor Grace Marie Ransom. Grace Marie—that name sounded so familiar . . .

Penciled at the bottom of the page was a note:

> "Hi Pam! I wanted to let you know that I now am serving a church! It all started when you prayed with me in our cabin at Camp Wesley Forest. I asked Jesus to be my Savior that night back during the summer of 5th grade. Now God has called me to pastoral ministry! I just wanted to say thank you. Love, G. Marie (Yorks) Ransom."

G. Marie Yorks . . . of course! I remembered her fresh honesty and enthusiasm as a camper. I had no idea God had called her to ministry. Now a whole congregation would benefit from her excitement about Jesus. Isn't it amazing how God took the seed of that simple devotional I shared and nurtured, watered and tended it till He harvested awesome fruit in G. Marie's life?

We just never know.

Prayer: Lord, I am humbled that you can use my efforts to produce fruit for your Kingdom. May my writing plant seeds of faith and water sprouts of belief. Amen.

Writing Application: Fertilizing, weeding, and dead-heading are also aspects of gardening. How might your writing be likened to one of the tasks usually associated with gardening?

H is for Hook: Writing to Catch a Reader

> "Jesus said to them, 'Come with me, and I will teach you to catch people.'"
>
> —Matthew 4:19

Read: Matthew 13:47

Have you ever gone fishing? My aunt Jan taught me that successful fishing is more than just good luck.

Knowledge of the sport makes the difference, starting with the right hook. Besides deciding whether a large or small hook is needed, line size, fish species, and type of bait also play a major role in hook selection.

Eva Shaw, writing instructor, says "hooks" are equally important in writing. In the case of a manuscript, a hook is an appealing opening sentence or paragraph that reels the reader in, reveals the subject and tone of a piece, and piques a reader's curiosity about what follows. Effective hooks will vary with the intended audience and subject matter.

Most people decide within the first few sentences whether or not they are going to continue reading. As writers for Jesus with a message of eternal importance, we don't want our readers to "get away". With just a few helpful tips we can craft successful hooks that will invite others to read on:

- Open with dialogue: "Your son is bleeding internally. What happened?" the doctor asked.

- Ask a thought-provoking question: "Did you know there are monsters in the Bible?"

- Begin with an action: "As Ernie swaggered in the church doors, Josh dialed 911."

- Define a term: "Sanctification is the ongoing process of becoming more Christ-like."

- Use tension-building description: "Sunlight filtered over the charred sanctuary."

- Quote a Scripture or person: "Bad companions ruin good character."

- Invite the reader to imagine: "Imagine learning you will have a baby in your nineties."

- Reveal a startling statistic: "Eighty percent of Americans hold no church affiliation."

- Throw out a challenge: "Want to overcome worry?"

Prayer: Lord, you know my desire is to bring others to you. Grant me the words to draw readers in, right from the beginning. Amen.

A to Z Devotions for Writers

Writing Application: Read the first page of ten of your favorite books. Write down the sentence(s) that "hooked" you.

I is for Inspiration: Writing Wellsprings

"Write, then, the things you see . . ."
—Revelation 1:19

Read: Habakkuk 2:2

A rare opportunity presented itself. With my family adventuring elsewhere, seven days of solitude stretched before me. I envisioned devotionals and articles flowing uninterrupted from my fingertips. I stared excitedly at the clean, white page on my computer, my heart full to the brim with longing to craft life-changing words.

Seconds lengthened from minutes to half an hour. The computer screen remained blank—as did my mind. I finally had the time and now I couldn't think of a thing to write about! I felt like Bastian fighting the obliterating force of "The Nothing" in the movie *The NeverEnding Story* (1984).

Finally, I did what I should have done first. "Lord, I set aside this time to write, but now I have no idea what to write about! Inspire me, Lord!" I prayed.

Pamela D. Williams

All writers face "The Nothing" at one time or another. Where do you turn for inspiration? You might want to try one of these simple suggestions for generating creative writing ideas:

- Prayerfully gaze out the window and watch for God's leading.
- Meditate on, ponder, pray over, and cross-reference Scripture.
- Browse journal entries to stir memories and brew ideas.
- Take a writers' field trip–visit a friend, check out a new store, go hiking, etc.
- Read. Stories, articles and poems by our favorite authors can spark our own imagination.
- Write from prompts. Writing exercises can be a springboard for stories.
- Take a writing course like the affordable ones offered at www.ed2go.com.
- Join a writers' group. When we get together with other writers we motivate one another.
- Respond to article and story call-outs posted on the Internet and in magazines.
- Peruse your quote file. Quotes can kindle a desire to express our thoughts on the subject.

A to Z Devotions for Writers

By traveling one or more of these avenues of inspiration we can cruise along on the writer's journey with plenty of fuel for stories, articles or whatever God calls us to write.

Prayer: Holy Spirit, when my screen remains blank, please breathe inspiration on the coals of my imagination so I can once again write for you. Amen.

Writing Application: Choose one of the avenues for generating inspiration and write a story or article.

J is for Journals: Writing from Day to Day

> "I looked at this, thought about it, and learned a lesson from it."
>
> —Proverbs 24:32

Read: Ecclesiastes 12:9-11

Midway along the raised walkway of Aldersgate Street, London, stands a bronze memorial flame inscribed with an excerpt from John Wesley's journal, dated May 24, 1738:

> "In the evening I went unwillingly to a society in Aldersgate Street, where one was reading Luther's preface to the Epistle to the Romans. About a quarter before nine, while he was describing the change which God works in the heart through faith in Christ, I felt my heart strangely warmed. I felt I did trust in Christ, Christ alone, for salvation; and an assurance was given me, that He had taken away my sins, even mine, and saved me from the law of sin and death."

While visiting this renowned site, tears of wonder blurred my vision. Wesley's words struck a chord in my soul, for they mirrored my own experience the Sunday morning I understood for the first time that "[God] saved us and called us to be His people, not because of what we have done, but because of His own purpose and grace. He gave us this grace by means of Christ Jesus . . ." (2 Timothy 1:9)

Like Wesley, a man plagued by self-doubt, we can't even imagine that our unassuming journal entries would ever be worthy of preservation on a street-side plaque. In fact, when it's time to write we wonder, "Is it really worth the effort to record my thoughts and perceptions from the day?"

However, my experience at Aldersgate Street confirms God can use the insights and observations that we scribble in private journals to renew His Spirit within the soul who stumbles across them—even centuries later!

Prayer: Lord, please use my heartfelt words to share your saving grace—even beyond the days allotted to me. Amen.

Writing Application: If you don't already have a journal, pick one up. A one-subject notebook will do. Choose a sentence from our Bible reading for today and write about how it spoke to you.

K is for Kindred: Writing Buddies

"People learn from one another just as iron sharpens iron."
—Proverbs 27:17

Read: Romans 15:14

With whom do you share kinship–that special connection stemming from like-minded beliefs and interests? My kindred spirits, (as Anne of Green Gables would call them), not only write, but share my Christian faith.

I found Christian kinship in my www.Ed2Go.com creative writing courses. Many fellow believers gravitate there, striving to become better scribes for Jesus. In "Write Your Life Story", classmates shared personal needs and prayer requests. Encouragement flowed from one writer to another. In this nurturing environment, everyone's writing blossomed and flourished.

I enjoyed a similar experience during a recent blogging challenge. Kindred spirits humbly admitted their vulnerabilities, boldly proclaimed the Good News about Jesus, and excitedly shared how they saw God working. Through comments, we cheered each other on and ended up developing lasting friendships.

Pamela D. Williams

Without a doubt, Christian writers' groups have provided the best place for me to gather with kindred spirits. I love the motivation to write, the encouragement to hone my craft, and the helpful critiques that I have received there. Local writers' groups afford the opportunity to meet face-to-face, forge friendships, and arrange to gather outside of the group meetings.

God's Word sheds light on why it is so important to gather with Christian writers:

- It is a place where we can receive correction for our work. (Proverbs 28:23)
- Two working together is more efficient than one. (Ecclesiastes 4:9)
- Jesus is present. (Matthew 18:20)
- We can encourage and help one another. (1 Thessalonians 5:11)
- We can share the fellowship of faith. (Hebrews 10:24-25)

Prayer: Thank you, Lord, for those who share my passion for writing and my love for you. Help me to encourage and challenge my fellow writers as we travel this path together. Amen.

Writing Application: Write a press release inviting others to your local writers' group. Include the benefits writers would gain from joining. If you are not yet involved with a Christian writers' group, write 100 words about why you need to find one. Then search the Internet, call local libraries, and scan the community events page of your newspaper for opportunities to gather with Christian writers.

L is for Light: Writing to Draw Others to Jesus

"**Y**ou are like light for the whole world."
—Matthew 5:14a

Read: Matthew 5:14-16

Turn on your porch light in the summer months and in a few moments all kinds of moths will automatically move toward the light. Look up at a street light and you will see them congregating. They flutter around our patio lights and frequent torch-lit garden parties.

Why do moths gravitate toward light? According to some entomology experts, the moths are seeking direction in the dark. Which explains why, in Matthew 5, Jesus compares his followers to light.

Acts 13:47 says the Lord has made us a light so that the whole world may be saved. Our spiritual light is not to be hidden away like a misplaced flashlight that we can't find when we need it. Our light is to be out there, readily shining where others can see it—where it will reveal the way to God.

As Christian writers we want our words to be like a porch light in summer—shining in the darkness, drawing our readers in, and inviting them to get to know Jesus. Our books, stories, poems—all that we write—can relate how God loves and cares for us and can attract those who are troubled, hurting, discouraged or searching.

Whether posted on our blog, published in a book, or sent to a friend in a letter, our written expressions of God's truths can illuminate His plan for forgiveness and a second chance for souls who desperately need and want a clean slate and new possibilities. We can offer them light for the dark places in their lives.

Jesus encouraged us to shine his light in this sin-darkened world and attract others to God. It is humbling to realize that our scribbled thoughts and scrawled ideas could one day light the way for others to find salvation through Jesus; that our words hold forth hope to world-weary travelers looking for the way to their spiritual home. Let's leave our lights on for them.

Prayer: Dear God, guide and direct the words that I write today. Infuse them with inspiration from your Spirit that they may light the path for readers who are searching for you. Amen.

Writing Application: Using crosswalk.com (or another Bible reference tool), conduct a search for the word "light" in the Bible. Choose one of the verses and journal how it speaks to your heart.

M is for Memoirs: Writing for the Next Generation

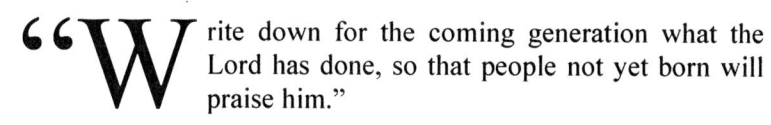

""Write down for the coming generation what the Lord has done, so that people not yet born will praise him."

—Psalm 102:18

Read: Psalm 22:30-31

"Believing is easy—when you're a kid," begins the "Believing" chapter of Allen Ewing's memoirs. Eager to pass on his faith to his family, Allen joined the writers' group at our church to garner some pointers. He discovered that recounting his rich, full life allowed him to highlight his spiritual milestones. The following is an excerpt from Allen's memoirs:

> "As I stood beside [my father's] casket, I reached out and touched his hand. I was startled. It was cold and hard, not soft and warm as it had always been. All of a sudden I realized that I was looking at a shell of what used to be my father. My dad was somewhere else and for the first time I truly understood the concept of 'spirit'."

Like Allen, we can plant seeds of faith in the hearts of family, friends, and even complete strangers when we scatter them throughout the fertile stories of day-to-day living. God's Holy Spirit will touch our words and transform them into channels of His love.

Must memoirs always take the form of a book? No, our memories, and our faith, can be passed from generation to generation in a variety of genres:

- Journaling
- Blogging
- Writing short stories or devotionals.
- Scrapbooking letters (both sent and received)
- Composing poems

Experiment till you find the best format for you. You will see how God's plan, rooted in your earliest days, has blossomed.

Prayer: Father, you know my deep desire is to plant seeds of faith in my loved ones. Show me how to embed the account of my spiritual journey into my memoirs so future generations can learn your truths. Amen.

Writing Application: Choose a favorite hymn or praise song. Perhaps it's one you sang in church or learned at camp. Was it a family favorite or is it one you came across on Christian radio? Play the song and allow it to transport you back to the moment in time you associate with it. Relive the emotions you felt. Write about where you were, what had happened that day, and why you were there. Vividly capture the moment for a future reader.

N is for No: Writing in the Face of Rejection

> "Now don't be discouraged, any of you. Do the work, for I am with you."
>
> —Haggai 2:4

Read: Philippians 3:12-13

In my favorite comic strip Snoopy stands by his mailbox reading a letter from a publisher: "Thank you for letting us read your autobiography. It's the worst book we have ever read. If you didn't live so far away we'd come and throw rocks at your mailbox."

Crushing words for most writers–but how does Snoopy react? He crumples the letter and tosses it over his shoulder. "Another form rejection letter," he thinks to himself.

Oh, to be that nonchalant about rejection!

My rejection notices from editors have arrived in various formats—short emails, fill-in-the-blank postcards, and form letters with applicable standard comments checked. But mostly, rejection has hidden in a bottomless abyss of silence.

How do writers handle rejection without becoming disheartened? As I studied the Snoopy comic strip, God reminded me of three scriptures to help gain perspective when editors say, "No":

1. Haggai 2:4 reminds us not to get discouraged. God called us to this writing venture and He will see us through. Rejection didn't discourage Snoopy and it need not discourage us.

2. Proverbs 15:32 advises us to accept correction. Though Snoopy's letter from the editor offered no helpful comments, sometimes editors will graciously take the time to explain the reasons for rejecting our work. We can always learn something from the submission process.

3. Philippians 3:12-13 urges us to forget what is behind and press on toward the goal. Keep writing. Where do we find Snoopy in the last frame? He's seated at his typewriter! Although his book was returned, he didn't lose his determination to write.

As I "keep on keeping on" with my writing, I am deeply grateful for the insights God shares with me through my craft—joys no editor or rejection slip can steal.

Prayer: God, when my hard work is not accepted, grant me the grace to handle the rejection in a way that both pleases you and fosters the most growth for me as a writer. Amen.

Writing Application: Our writing always benefits from a little breathing time. Choose a piece you wrote that was rejected by an editor or that you gave up on. Pray over the manuscript; then, with God's direction, rework it.

O is for Overcome: Writing, Over, Under, and Through

"**D**o not be afraid - I am with you! I am your God - let nothing terrify you!"

—Isaiah 41:10a

Read: Ephesians 6:11-18

At times, fear, self-doubt, and other obstacles loom larger than life for writers, but we can overcome. With God's encouragement and inspiration we can prevail over writer's block, expel the blues of rejection, and squelch reticence to market our work. Yes, we can banish paralyzing fear and even defeat self-doubt!

How? Hebrews 4:12 tells us "The word of God is alive and active." Comparable to wielding a sword, turning to Scripture can slice through the obstructions that barricade our path to creativity.

Self-doubt tops the obstacle list for most writers. However, Philippians 4:13 assures us that we can do all things through Christ! Praise God for His vote of confidence in us!

Do fears disable your creativity or cause you to procrastinate? 2 Timothy 1:7 reminds us that timidity does not come from God. Instead He fills us with power, love, and self-discipline to overcome all our fears, including those concerning our writing.

Suffering with writer's block? The Bible contains inspired stories of courage, romance, and sacrifice. Poetry, narration and dialogue fill the pages. When we read God's Word, the Author of life can set our hearts on fire again and motivate us to write for Him.

Do you feel a reticence about marketing your work? "How can others call to God for help if they have not believed? And how can they believe if they have not heard the message? And how can they hear if the message is not proclaimed?" (Romans 10:14) No one can benefit from our God-inspired stories if our only reader is the virus protection program on our computer.

Prayer: Lord, you have called me to this writing life. Don't allow obstacles, real or imagined, to keep me from answering your call. Amen.

Writing Application: Make a list of your fears about writing. Allow God to arm you against them by searching a concordance for Scriptures to address each obstacle on your list.

P is for Prayer: Writing in the Power of Prayer

"**D**o all this in prayer, asking for God's help. Pray on every occasion, as the Spirit leads. For this reason keep alert and never give up; pray always for all God's people."

—Ephesians 6:18

Read: Philippians 4:6

"Well, Lord, here goes," I think to myself, my cursor poised over the send button and my trigger finger at the ready. I feel a clutching in my stomach and my neck muscles tightening. Excitement and fear, anxiety and relief crowd around as I click the mouse to email a manuscript to an editor. My knees literally shake when I stand up afterward, the need to stretch overwhelming me. If I had obeyed Ephesians 6:18 instead of offering a cursory, "Here goes!" much of the drama would have been relieved.

Writing is a vital ministry that requires God's guidance from beginning to end. A pastor cannot preach effective sermons without thoroughly praying about them. Youth leaders cannot effectively minister unless they have sought God's direction for their leadership. Writers are no different. For our writing to be effective, it must be God-inspired and God-blessed.

Pamela D. Williams

So, how do we bathe our manuscripts in prayer? Start by thanking God for this incredible gift. Request God's guidance in keeping the piece scriptural. Ask, "What would you like me to write today, Lord? Who will be reading this? What slant do you want me to take?"

Since God inspires what we write, we need to thank Him when an article is finished. Pray about where to submit it; ask Him to speak to the heart of the editor who will receive it.

If a story is rejected, turn to God for the revisions; when it is accepted give Him the praise and ask Him to touch the lives of those who will read the finished work.

These suggestions connect us with the Author of our faith, open our eyes to His handiwork in all phases of our writing, and fill our hearts with gratitude. As with every God-given gift, writing carries the responsibility of using it to draw others to Jesus, so God's command to "Pray continually," (1 Thessalonians 5:17) just makes sense.

Prayer: Father, help me not to forge ahead with my writing on my own. Guide and direct every word that I pen. Amen.

Writing Application: Set aside 15 minutes to prayerfully brain-storm. Ask God to make clear what He wants you to write. Jot down the ideas. If you are in the middle of a project, allow God to direct your thoughts on how to proceed with it.

Q is for Quiet: Writing in the Secret Place

"But [Jesus] would go away to lonely places, where he prayed."

—Luke 5:16

Read: 1 Kings 19:11-13.

"In the Secret"

by

Andy Park

In the secret, in the quiet place,

In the stillness You are there.

In the secret,

In the quiet hour I wait, only for You,

Cause, I want to know You more.

I love this song. But the truth is I have trouble sitting quietly. When I pray, I want to tell Jesus all my problems, ask for solutions, and then rush off and do something—without waiting for Him to speak.

However, if we desire to serve God with our gift of writing, Psalm 46:10 offers us profound advice: "Be still and know that I am God."

As writers who truly want to know God's will for our work, perhaps we need to look more closely at quietness as a way to open a channel for us to listen for God's leading. We can benefit, as Jesus did, by finding a "lonely" place to meet God.

For some of us silence may seem an uncomfortable waste of precious time. However, quieting ourselves stops activity, hushes noise, and calms our minds so we can hear God's soft whisper. Since God often speaks through our minds rather than our ears, we need to center our thoughts and close our mouths. Our goal for quiet moments is to listen for God's answers.

In quiet God speaks. We can put distractions aside, tune in to Him and breathe in His love. Quiet allows God to renew and equip us to minister to others through our writing.

Can you hear Him now?

Prayer: Lord, I want your input in my writing. Help me to quietly listen for your direction before planning or acting on my writing. Amen.

Writing Application: How can we practice quietude without adding stress to our lives? Simply spend a few silent, listening moments following our prayers for each stage of our writing. Keeping a pen and paper handy will enable us to jot down the responses and nudges with which God blesses us.

H

R is for Reading: Writing Requires Reading

"**I**ntelligent people are always eager and ready to learn."
—Proverbs 18:15

Read: Proverbs 2:2-4

As I opened the desk drawer the pastel drawing of a little peasant girl, nose-to-beak with a huge white goose, caught my eye. I picked up the Precious Moments bookmark, a pleasant reminder of one of the loves of my life—reading.

Experts say that writers must be avid readers in order to write well. How does God use reading, whether it is novels, newspapers, or non-fiction, to improve our writing skills?

- Author and business owner Corey Blake says, "The act of reading exceptional writing is an injection of stem cells directly to your imagination. Great writing has a literal way of activating new pathways in your brain and opening up areas of new thought."

- Mary Jaksch, Chief Editor of the blog "Write to Done" notes, "Beyond reading for pleasure, a good writer also reads with an eye for the writing. And many times that writer doesn't even realize he's doing it. . . What we learn as readers, we use as writers. . . Over time, our writing becomes in some ways a compilation of all the things we've learned as readers, blended together in our own unique recipe."

- Writer Jeff Goins advises, "As a writer, you'll find yourself hitting plateaus and roadblocks . . . actually running out of words, if you're not regularly being challenged through reading new things. [Reading] is an important step to becoming a good writer. . . Read . . . to glean new ideas, to learn new words, to fall back in love with language."

Proverbs 27:17 says we learn from one another. What does God want you to glean from what you are reading? Are you setting aside time to replenish creativity, stretch your vocabulary, and view the world through different eyes. Will you join me for a read-fest?

Prayer: Thank you, Lord, for inspiring a plethora of books, articles, and poetry. Please grant me the time to read and savor some of these delicious morsels and use them to improve my skills as a writer. Amen.

Writing Application: Take a few moments to enjoy that new novel you downloaded, peruse a few news articles, or catch up on some blogs you've been longing to read. Keep paper and pencil handy to note writing ideas or tips that God points out as you read.

S is for Submissions: Writing for Publication

> "What I am telling you in the dark you must repeat in broad daylight, and what you have heard in private you must announce from the housetops."
> —Matthew 10:27

Read: Acts 1:8

"I am only writing these stories for my kids."

"I could never get published."

"I don't want to submit and fail."

"My stuff is too boring for others to read."

Does that sound like the "housetops" to you? We exert a lot of time and creativity in crafting a story. However, many talented writers dismiss their efforts and make similar comments.

Writers often lack the confidence to submit their work for publication. I have to admit that even after years of submitting, pushing "send" to email a story to a publisher or editor still makes me sweaty and shaky. I wonder,

"Have I missed a grammar mistake? Can my story really compete with the thousands of other submissions?"

When I suggest publication to a fellow writer, his/her insecurities, like mine, usually surface. The person either laughs nervously or waves away the idea as impossible. Even writing just for family or sharing one of our stories with a close friend can cause butterflies in our stomachs.

Prolific author, Lee Roddy says:

> "If it is God's will for us to write, then it's logical that publication should eventually follow. After all, an unfinished manuscript cannot change lives. Even a finished one cannot minister in a drawer or filing cabinet. Only in published form can a story go where you and I will never go, to people we will never meet. Only in published form can our writing make a difference in eternity."

Roddy's statement reflects Scripture. "No one lights a lamp and puts it under a basket. Instead, everyone who lights a lamp puts it on a lamp stand. Then its light shines on everyone in the house." (Matthew 5:15)

God doesn't want us to keep His message to ourselves. Where is He calling you to share yours?

Prayer: Father God, grant me the wisdom to know which manuscripts to submit for publication, and grant me the confidence to push "Send". Amen.

Writing Application: Find an appropriate market for one of your pieces by researching online or in one of the writers' market guides. Polish the piece to suit the publisher's guidelines and have it critiqued by other writers. Submit it to God's will and then send it to the market you chose.

T is for Testimony: Writing to Witness

"**B**e ready at all times to answer anyone who asks you to explain the hope you have in you."
—1 Peter 3:15

Read: Acts 22:15

"Anybody have any questions?" Pastor Ed Cope asked after sharing God's plan of salvation with the 4th through 6th grade boys and girls gathered in the camp lodge for devotions.

Frantically waving her hand about six inches from Ed's face, one camper said, "When I get home, should I tell my parents?"

"If you asked Jesus to forgive your sins and come into your life, wait to share the news until your parents comment on the positive changes they've seen in you since camp," advised Pastor Cope. "When we tell others what Jesus has done in our lives, we are His witnesses. In a court room, individuals can't just run up and take the witness stand. A witness is asked to give testimony."

Pamela D. Williams

Have you ever been asked about your faith, about how it affects your reaction to what life throws your way? God instructs us to be prepared to explain the hope we have. As writers we wield an advantage—we can prepare to share our testimony by writing out the story of how we trusted in Jesus as our Savior. Whether it is a chapter in our memoirs, a letter to a friend, or a magazine article, our testimony personalizes the Gospel and gives irrefutable proof of the change Jesus can bring about in a life.

Prayer: Jesus, nothing adequately expresses my thanks to you for your sacrifice. Help me to set aside the time to write down my story of how faith in you has changed my life. Direct my words that they may one day guide another soul to you. Amen.

Writing Application: You can start writing your testimony simply by answering these questions:

1. Before I trusted Jesus, what was my mental image of God? What struggles did I face? What was important to me?

2. When I encountered Jesus, how did I come to realize God really loved me? How did I become convinced that Jesus' death on the cross paid the price for me?

3. Now that I am living for Jesus, what am I doing to further develop my relationship with him? What changes have occurred in my basic outlook on life?

U is for Urgent: Writing is Crucial

> "Hear what God says: 'When the time came for me to show you favor, I heard you; when the day arrived for me to save you, I helped you.' Listen! This is the hour to receive God's favor; today is the day to be saved!"
> —2 Corinthians 6:2

Read: Luke 10:38-42

Like many women, my daughter struggles to balance a full-time job, maintain a home, and still spend time with her kids. Often when asked how her weekend went, she laments, "Well, I cleaned."

Unexpectedly one Saturday, her answer differed. "I am packing the car for a quick trip to the lake. Cleaning the house just doesn't seem as crucial when the kids need my attention so much more."

Convicted by our conversation, I prayerfully asked God to reveal the things in my life that I was granting unmerited urgency. God reminded me of the account of Jesus' visit with Mary and Martha. Martha felt it was her duty to rush around preparing a meal. Reprimanding her, Jesus quite plainly told Martha she was missing out on what was really important at that moment.

God opened my eyes to see that I am much like Martha when it comes to my writing—I allowed other things to come first. Often I do unnecessary housework instead of settling down to write. I have wasted hours shopping online for a better price on a birthday gift when I could have been researching markets for my work.

Thankfully, our forgiving God re-emphasized for me the urgency of writing. He has shown me that my writing is a ministry that He can use to draw others into a right relationship with Him and to help Christians grow spiritually—responsibilities far more crucial in the light of eternity than an immaculate house or a fantastic bargain.

Prayer: Father God, I long for you to keep me from paying attention to what is worthless. Help me to see the urgency of writing for you. Amen.

Writing Application: Unless we make time to write, our writing will never reach the potential God intended. Where does writing fall on your list of "Things To-Do"? In what position do you sense God sees your writing? Prayerfully note three practical ways to devote more time to your writing and then implement them.

V is for Voice: Writing from Within

"You created every part of me . . ."
— Psalm 139:13

Read: Psalm 139

As I walked in the sanctuary of early morning, a wide variety of birds were singing their pure thanks for being alive. Cardinals, robins, sparrows, finches, crows, blue jays, doves, chickadees and wrens lifted their distinctive voices, creating a chorus of glorious praise to God. I couldn't help but join them!

Just as God gave each species of bird a distinguishing voice, so God gifts each writer. As an extension of our individual personalities, our writer's voice combines word choices, style, preferred punctuation, use of dialogue, etc. in a manner that naturally surfaces when we relax and let it flow.

Joyce Parker, writer for Wiki.answers.com urges us to write how we speak, as if we are just talking to a friend in our living room, not trying to write in a certain style or using "fancy" words and phrases, (unless we normally talk that way). Writing honestly, we can let our real emotions show through and include them in our stories.

Pamela D. Williams

In my writer's group we often email pieces back and forth to be critiqued. I remember the day Brianna pointed out to me that my writer's voice was instantly recognizable, "When I read your meditation, Pam, I would have known it was yours even without your name at the bottom. I could 'hear' your voice in my head, speaking the words."

God calls us to write in the unique voice He has given us in order to reach a multitude of people. What one writer does not or cannot articulate another can and does. Out of His unending love for all people, God uses every resource available to connect with those who don't yet know Him. Our voice may be just the one that can touch a particular reader's heart.

Prayer: Lord, I thank you for the inimitable writing voice you have given me. Help me not to mimic anyone else's voice, but instead allow you to nurture mine. Amen.

Writing Application: Write down three words that others use to describe you. Are you open, honest, and frank? Are you warm, accepting and comforting? With your characteristics in mind, look at several of your latest writing efforts. Highlight the phrases that voice your personality.

W is for Words: Writing Wields Power

"What you say can preserve life or destroy it; so you must accept the consequences of your words."
—Proverbs 18:21

Read: Ephesians 4:29

"Sticks and stones may break my bones, but words can never hurt me," we chanted on the playground in elementary school when despicable boys would call skinny girls "Bird Legs", or when they laughingly pointed at Anna and yelled, "Run! It's 'Cooties'!"

Did we really think words couldn't hurt? Had we actually believed that old adage? Anna certainly didn't. Fifty years later, I can still see her pain-filled eyes brimming with tears.

Perhaps we chanted that old cliché one too many times, for incredibly, though words are the building materials of the writer's craft, we often view what we write as trivial and ineffective. We wonder at times why anyone would want to read our words.

God, on the other hand, considers words vitally important—so much so in fact, that he refers to Jesus as "the Word", with a capital W, seven times in the first fourteen verses of John 1.

Despite what we tried to convince our tormenters, (and ourselves), in grade school, words do wield power. Although many of us have experienced their power to hurt, words also have the power to heal, reconcile, encourage, empower, and save.

Notes of encouragement, poems of tribute, insightful comments on blogs, devotionals full of truth—God can use our words to comfort hearts, open minds, and transform lives. God knows the importance and the power of words. Right, Anna?

Prayer: Lord, forgive me for taking so lightly this gift of words that you have given me. Help me to seek your guidance in all that I write. Guard and empower my words as a ministry for you. I ask this in the name of Jesus—the Word. Amen.

Writing Application: When have words been used to hurt you? How did you handle the hurt? Do they still knot up your stomach and steal your confidence? Write the words on a piece of paper. Pray over the words and your memory of the incident. Ask God to help you to forgive the one who spoke them and to overcome any lingering negative reactions you carry. Then put the paper through a shredder, crumple it up and forcefully throw it away, or take it outside in a discarded can and light it. Those words no longer have power over you. God gives the victory! Praise His name.

X is for Explicable*: Writing Understandably

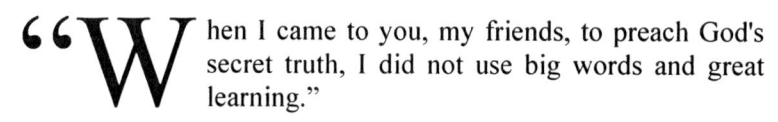

> "When I came to you, my friends, to preach God's secret truth, I did not use big words and great learning."
>
> —1 Corinthians 2:1

Read: 1 Corinthians 1:17

"Be sure to X out of all programs before running the antivirus software," the website instructed.

"GTG TTYL XOXO," the text read.

"1 capsule 3x per day," the doctor had noted on Amy's discharge papers.

"I feel the store should not carry movies rated X," Don told the manager of the rental store.

"The dimensions of the table are 42" x 22" x 36"," the Craigslist ad stated.

As we can see in the examples above, X is often used as a "code" word that means different things depending on the vocabulary of a particular subject or group of people. While X sends a kiss when we text "XOXO", it indicates "times" in a prescription. If we are not familiar with the jargon, we may not be sure what x might mean.

As Christian writers we sometimes slip into lingo that is referred to as Christian-ese. We throw around words like "saved by grace", "born again", "washed in the blood", "baptized in the Spirit", "fruit of the Spirit", "walk by faith", "prayed the prayer", etc. Occasionally we even use codes, like "PTL", "IXOYE", "XMAS", or "IHS".

The problem is this ambiguous language is only correctly understood by those who were raised in the church. It is unproductive when writing for those who have not yet encountered Christ. Yet many of us continually fall back on these over-used phrases rather than taking the extra time and effort to express ourselves in easily explicable terms that the un-churched will understand.

God has driven this point home to me on several occasions since our son married a young woman who was born and raised in China. It is difficult for us to explain the relationship we have with Jesus. Although she sees the difference our Christian beliefs make in our lives, it is challenging for us to put those beliefs into words that have meaning to someone with a faith base that differs from ours. Writers face the same challenge.

Prayer: Father, heighten my sensitivity to the needs of my readers and guide me in how to clearly share your truths. Amen.

Writing Application: Make a list of words you commonly use in talking about your faith. Next to each word write synonyms that could be substituted in order in ensure greater comprehension for all your readers.

*Yes, I admit. My "X" word cheats a bit. ☺

Y is for Yearn: Writing Goals

"Happy are those whose greatest desire [yearning] is to do what God requires; God will satisfy them fully!"

—Matthew 5:6

Read: Psalm 37:4

What do you yearn for as a writer? Do you crave the ability to write in a way that will touch hearts for Jesus? Is your greatest desire to share your spiritual journey with your family? Do you long to be published so others can learn from the truths God has whispered to your heart? Is it your vision to become a full-time writer?

It's important for us to take the time to ask ourselves what our purpose, dreams, and goals are for our writing. Why? Because our purpose will sustain us when we feel like we can't write another word; our goals will reveal the strides we have made with our writing; our dreams will motivate us to take our writing to the next level.

Author J.W. Allen says, "[Setting goals] is especially important for writers, since so much of what we do requires self-discipline and long-term commitment, often with no immediate tangible reward to prod us further."

Very true, I've discovered. The initial writing of the devotionals for this book flowed smoothly and swiftly. However, about a third of the way through the editing, every devotional started to sound the same to me. I took a break, telling myself I would get back to it in a few weeks. Eighteen months later I attended a writers' seminar and felt God nudge me to push ahead with the project.

Freelance writers rarely work with deadlines looming or a taskmaster breathing down our necks—which sounds great until we hit a snag in a storyline or get bogged down in editing, like I did, with no one to offer suggestions or cheer us on.

Holly Tucker, writer and editor, suggests setting weekly writing goals and sharing them with a fellow writer or writing group. This will help keep us accountable and also will provide welcome encouragement and support.

Pray: Lord, overhaul my yearnings for my writing and make my desires line up with yours. Amen.

Writing Application: Take the time to be alone in a quiet place and sort out your greatest desires for you writing. Write these yearnings down. Pray over them. What is God saying to you about what you are longing for? Share your goals with a writer friend or writers' group.

Z is for Zest: Writing with Pizazz

"*Y*ou are like salt for the whole human race. . ."
—Matthew 5:13

Read: Psalm 34:8

"Zest!" read the sign above the entryway. "Sounds interesting," I said, smiling at my two friends. "Let's go in."

We discovered the eclectic store while wandering Main Street in Lititz, PA following a writers' workshop. Excited by the information the speaker shared that morning, we were ambling along jabbering like a trio of magpies— until the store name "Zest!" caught our attention and lured us in.

"Interesting" turned out to be an understated description. As their website will tell you, the owners, Jim and Sharon Landis, are enthusiastic foodies. And it shows! The Landis's filled Zest! with quality domestic and imported ingredients, unique gifts, and a wide assortment of new and vintage gadgets sure to excite fellow foodies. We now understood the "Zest!" moniker.

Doesn't zest describe what Jesus encouraged His followers to offer the world in Matthew 5:13? As Christian writers, shouldn't we present our readers with quality workmanship, unique perspectives on a wide assortment of topics, and a contagious enthusiasm?

Author and friend, Virginia Jelinek reminded me that this God-flavored zest doesn't necessarily refer only to what we write for Christian publications. Secular writing by Christian authors can reach a diverse audience.

How can we covertly sprinkle the zest of Jesus in the writing we do for the secular markets?

1. Pray for, and follow, the leading of the Holy Spirit.
2. Incorporate characters with Christian convictions.
3. Express thankfulness, compassion, honesty, and integrity.
4. Handle sensitive subjects with extra care and delicate tact.
5. Keep family-friendly values in mind.

In the same way that the zest of a lemon enhances the flavors of food, the thrill and joy of following Jesus can so pepper our writing that others will want to taste and see that the Lord is good!

Prayer: Lord Jesus, please infuse my manuscript with your zest so that my words will cause my readers to hunger and thirst to know you more. Amen.

Writing Application: Pull out a secular piece you have written. Using a highlighter, underline the specific lines where your Christianity is latent. What techniques did you use to flavor your secular writing with the zest of the gospel?

ABOUT THE AUTHOR

Pamela Williams is a pastor's wife, mother and grandmother. She received her B.A. in English from Shippensburg University and has been freelance writing for nearly twenty years.

Pam's stories and articles have been published in print and online magazines, including TravelingMom.com, Live, Wesleyan Life, Upper Room, The Secret Place, Mature Years, Catholic Digest, Vista and more.

Six books in the *Chicken Soup for the Soul* series contain Pam's stories, as well as CSS Publishing's anthology, *Traveling Calvary's Road* (2007). CSS Publishing also released Pam's church and community resource book, *Baccalaureate: Guidelines for Inspirational Worship Services to Honor Graduates* (2008).

Out of her passion to help other writers become all that God is calling them to be, Pam birthed 1st Writes, an inspiration and feedback group for Christian writers in the Chambersburg, Pennsylvania area. Pam encourages authors to view their writings as a way to fulfill Jesus' Great Commission. As a member of 1st Writes, Pam posts on the 1st Writes collective blog at www.1stwrites.blogspot.com.

Pamela D. Williams

On her blog, 2 Encourage (www.pameladwilliams.blogspot.com), Pam posts devotions, poetry, stories and links to inspire and motivate anyone who is walking life's path with Jesus.

CPSIA information can be obtained at www.ICGtesting.com
Printed in the USA
BVOW04s1351170813

328623BV00001B/70/P

9 781936 746521